What Good Is an A?

amicus
readers

1

by Marie Powell

Say Hello to Amicus Readers.

You'll find our helpful dog, Amicus, chasing a ball—to let you know the reading level of a book.

1

Learn to Read
Frequent repetition, high frequency words, and close photo-text matches introduce familiar topics and provide ample support for brand new readers.

2

Read Independently
Some repetition is mixed with varied sentence structures and a select amount of new vocabulary words are introduced with text and photo support.

3

Read to Know More
Interesting facts and engaging art and photos give fluent readers fun books both for reading practice and to learn about new topics.

Amicus Readers are published by Amicus
P.O. Box 1329, Mankato, MN 56002
www.amicuspublishing.us

Library of Congress Cataloging-in-Publication Data

Powell, Marie, 1958- author.
  What good is an A? / by Marie Powell.
     pages cm. -- (Vowels)
  Summary: " Beginning readers are introduced to the vowel A and its sounds and uses."-- Provided by publisher.
  ISBN 978-1-60753-708-3 (library binding)
  ISBN 978-1-60753-812-7 (ebook)
  1. Vowels--Juvenile literature. 2. Phonetics--Juvenile literature. I. Title.
  P233.P69 2015
  428.1--dc23
                          2014045355

Photo Credits: Thinkstock, cover, 1; Roman Samokhin/Shutterstock Images, 3; Wong Sze Yuen/Shutterstock Images, 5, 16 (top left); Monkey Business Images/Shutterstock Images, 6, 8-9, 13; Z. Kruger/Shutterstock Images, 10; Irina Barcari/Shutterstock Images, 14; Shutterstock Images, 16 (top right); Romiana Lee/Shutterstock Images, 16 (bottom right); Moiseev Vladislav/Thinkstock, 16 (bottom left)

Produced for Amicus by The Peterson Publishing Company and Red Line Editorial.

Editor Jenna Gleisner
Designer Craig Hinton

Printed in Malaysia
10 9 8 7 6 5 4 3 2 1

What good is an **A**? **A** is a vowel, like E, I, O, U, and Y. What sound does **A** make?

A can have a long sound, like in the word cake. Amy ate cake.

A can have a short sound. Snack has the short A sound. Allen had a snack.

<u>A</u> can start a word.

<u>A</u>ndy <u>a</u>te <u>a</u>n <u>a</u>pple.

<u>A</u> can be in the middle of a word. M<u>a</u>ndy put j<u>a</u>m on her p<u>a</u>nc<u>a</u>kes tod<u>a</u>y.

11

A can be at the end of a word. Kayla asked her mom to make her a tuna sandwich.

A can even be **a** word by itself. Eli packed **a** sandwich and **a** banana for lunch.
A makes all kinds of words.

Vowel: A

Which words have a long **A** sound?

Which words have a short **A** sound?

Amy

jam

apple

cake